WORLD'S GREATEST ATHLETES

SURFING STARS

By Ellen Labrecque

The Child's World
www.childsworld.com

Published in the United States of America by The Child's World®
P.O. Box 326 • Chanhassen, MN 55317-0326
800-599-READ • www.childsworld.com

ACKNOWLEDGMENTS

The Child's World®: Mary Berendes, Publishing Director

Produced by Shoreline Publishing Group LLC
President / Editorial Director: James Buckley, Jr.
Designer: Tom Carling, carlingdesign.com
Assistant Editors: Jim Gigliotti, Ellen Labrecque

Photo Credits
Cover: Corbis.
Interior: All by Corbis except for Covered Images/Cestari: 25;
Covered Images/Tostee: 27; Getty Images: 11, 16, 23.

LIBRARY OF CONGRESS
CATALOGING-IN-PUBLICATION DATA

Labrecque, Ellen.
  Surfing stars / by Ellen Labrecque.
    p. cm. — (The world's greatest athletes)
  Includes bibliographical references and index.
  ISBN-13: 978-1-59296-793-3 (library bound : alk. paper)
  ISBN-10: 1-59296-793-0 (library bound : alk. paper)
 1. Surfing—Juvenile literature. 2. Surfers—Biography—Juvenile
literature. I. Title. II. Series.

GV839.5.L33 2007
797.3'20922—dc22
[B]

2006031555

CONTENTS

Hawaii: Home of Surfing

SURFING IS AN ANCIENT PART OF THE HAWAIIAN islands, but British explorer James Cook in 1779 was the first Westerner to witness it. In a journal, a member of Cook's team wrote about watching the natives ride the ocean waves on wooden boards.

However, Cook's arrival almost drowned the sport. Diseases brought by the Europeans killed thousands of Hawaiians. More and more Europeans followed Cook's crew to the islands, and they encouraged natives to work, rather than surf.

A group of hard-core surfers on Waikiki Beach near Honolulu kept the sport alive through the years, however. One of those devoted surfers was Duke Kahanamoku. After becoming world-famous by winning gold medals in swimming at the 1912

This statue on Waikiki Beach honors swimming champion and surfing ambassador Duke Kahanamoku (inset).

Olympics (he ended up with three more golds in his Olympic career), Duke traveled the world. Wherever he went, he demonstrated surfing, spreading the sport to beach cities from California to Australia.

Today, millions of people surf for fun, while pro surfers compete for big money in Association of Surfing Professionals (ASP) contests all over the world. The competitors are judged on how well they do tricks while riding their boards. At the end of the tour, the world champion is crowned.

This book celebrates the greatest surfers in the world today, **heirs** to the legacy of the ancient Hawaiians.

CHAPTER 1

Slater Shreds—Others Follow

THINK YOU HAVE TO SEARCH THE WORLD (OR GO to Hawaii) to find the best surfer ever? Think again. The top surfer on the planet was born in Cocoa Beach, Florida, on February 11, 1972. His name is Kelly Slater.

"Kelly Slater means to surfing what Michael Jordan means to basketball, what Tiger Woods means to golf," professional surfer C.J. Hobgood told *Sports Illustrated For Kids*. "'Everything' would be a good word [for what Slater means to the sport]."

Kelly began surfing when he was just five years old after watching his father and older brother take to the waves. In 1980, when he was eight, he entered his first contest and won. This was the first of many surfing wins in his awesome career.

During a 2006 event in California, Kelly Slater performs a cutback move, changing direction on the wave.

The rising star turned pro in 1990 and by 1992, he became the youngest surfer (at age 20) to win a world championship. From 1994 to 1998, Slater whipped off five straight titles. He also became surfing's biggest celebrity. Fans mobbed him everywhere he went.

He never had a second to himself. All the attention overwhelmed Kelly. In 1998, at age 26 and at the height of his career and popularity, he retired from surfing. But after three years away from the sport, the lure of the ocean proved too much to keep Slater away and he "un-retired" in 2002. By 2005, he was

Like other top pro surfers, Kelly earns money by winning, but also by wearing the logos of sponsors.

back to world championship form and won his record seventh title. At age 33, he was the oldest surfer ever to win the world championship.

"This was probably my most complete win," Slater told *Transworld Surf* magazine about his seventh title. "I feel like I'm bringing the pieces of my life together."

Kelly won two of the first six events of 2005 and finished in the top five in three others. At 34, Slater kept the party going and added to his record with his eighth world title in 2006. He doesn't know how much longer he'll surf but he knows there are still waves to surf . . . and events to win.

If there is any pro surfer who can compete with Slater, it's Andy Irons. Andy was born on July 24, 1978, in Hanalei, Kauai, Hawaii. Andy's dad, Phil, was a former professional surfer. Phil bought Andy and Andy's younger brother Bruce (also a pro surfer) their first board when Andy was eight and Bruce was seven.

"On Christmas morning we discovered a pair of surfboards under the tree," Andy told *Sports Illustrated*. "That afternoon we were in the waves having a blast."

Andy competed in his first contest at age 10.

In his 12 seasons of pro surfing (through 2006), Kelly Slater has won 33 surfing events and more than $1.4 million in prize money.

He began competing outside of Hawaii during his teenage years. Fans of the sports began calling him "The Next Kelly Slater." When Andy surfed, he reached crazy heights, and he could also stay on his board while riding some of the toughest waves. In 1998, at age 20, Andy **qualified** for the pro tour. By 2002, he had won his first world title.

Andy won the world title again in 2003, when he nudged out Slater in the final competition of the season. Irons won again in 2004, while Slater finished third. In 2005, Slater regained his crown, and the competition remains as intense as ever.

Bruce Irons was born just sixteen months after his older bro. Like Andy, Bruce grew up surfing almost every day. The ocean was his second home.

"Every day, same thing," Bruce and Andy's mom, Danielle, said about her boys' younger years. "School, surf, homework, dinner, sleep."

Although both brothers love surfing equally, they each have their own style when they hit the waves in competition. Andy is more serious in the water and focuses more on competition. When Bruce surfs, he is more of a daredevil.

"[Bruce] was more mysterious, " said their mom

in 2002. "Even now, he catches a wave and no one knows what he is going to do with it."

Bruce started competing on the tour in 2003. Although he hasn't had nearly the success his brother has had, he is still thought of as one of the best free surfers on the planet.

"If you're out free surfing—you know, without the clock [normally used during ASP events], when you can go for it more?" said 2000 world champion

Nice job, bro! Andy Irons (left) and brother Bruce finished first and third, respectively, at this 2006 event in Hawaii.

Bobby Martinez is a star on the rise, with his eyes on the world title.

Sunny Garcia. "Well, I don't know if Bruce isn't better than Andy."

Bobby Martinez is another American surfer who can compete with the likes of the Irons brothers and Kelly Slater. Bobby is the youngest of the four stars. He was born May 26, 1982, in Santa Barbara, California. His first year on the tour was not until 2006, but the rookie quickly made waves. He was ranked fourth in the world in 2006, and he already landed his first tour victory—the Billabong Pro Tahiti.

"It is all happening so fast," Bobby told *Surfing Magazine* about his rise to stardom.

Who knows whether Bobby will someday be as good as the Irons brothers, or for that matter Kelly Slater. But, really, it doesn't matter to fans. The thrill is in watching all four cruise the ocean waves, ride after ride, as their fans cheer and their fellow surfers look on in wonder.

Big Wave Rider

Laird Hamilton is the world's most daring surfer. The 6'3", 215-pound legend grew up on the Hawaiian islands of Oahu and Kauai. He doesn't compete on the pro tour. Instead, Laird, age 42, spends all his time surfing on the most dangerous water in the world. He is towed out by a watercraft to monster waves at offshore reefs. At just the right time, Laird is released into waves that reach 50 feet high. One false move and Laird could die.

Laird isn't just a surfer. He is an all-around waterman. In addition to surfing, he sails, paddleboards, kayaks, jet skis. Name a water activity, and Laird probably does it.

One of Laird's most famous surfing rides took place on August 17, 2000, way off the shore of Teahupoo, Tahiti. The waves there are considered the biggest and most violent waves in the world. Hamilton was so moved by the experience afterwards, he cried. Laird calls riding monster waves such as these the "ultimate sensation."

So what is next for the world's best big wave surfer? "Bigger, higher, faster," Laird says.

Mick Fanning performs a kickout move, reaching the top of a wave and then turning the nose of his board back to the wave.

CHAPTER 2

The Wide World of Surf Stars

HIT ANY BEACH AROUND THE WORLD, AND CHANCES are you'll find a surfer or two catching some waves. But try to find a surfer who makes you say "Wow!" and it isn't as easy. Mick Fanning of Australia is one of those "Wow!" surfers. He has bleached blond hair and surfs so fast, his nickname is "White Lightning." His name could also be the Comeback Kid.

Mick was born June 13, 1981, in Sydney, Australia. He grew up surfing, and turned pro in 2002. He finished fourth on the ASP Tour in 2003, and 2004 was supposed to be his biggest season yet. But, while surfing off the coast of Indonesia, Mick crashed. He suffered a horrible **hamstring** injury that forced him to the sidelines for the entire season. Mick took this crash as **motivation** to work twice as hard to get back

Mick's skills took him from Down Under to a spot among the world's best.

to top form. He changed his diet by cutting out junk food and trained harder than he ever had before. The hard work paid off. Mick won the first two events of the 2005 season and finished fourth overall. He remained among the world's best in 2006. Although it was tough for Mick to miss a whole year of competition, he also thinks the accident happened for a reason.

"It really brought my passion back for surfing," Mick told *Surfer* Magazine.

Fellow Aussie Taj Burrow is another surfer from **Down Under** who makes fans say, "Wow!" Taj was born on June 2, 1978, in Busselton, Western Australia. He grew up near some of the most surf-rich water in the world. Taj excelled at the sport from the moment he dipped his toes into the water. He won his first competition when he was just nine years old—at an 18-and-under contest. He turned pro in 1998 and was named Rookie of the Year. In 1999, Taj finished second in the world standings. Burrow is known on the tour for the **big air** he gets on tricks. Now, he has his sights on only one thing: a World Championship crown.

"Confidence is everything," Taj said. "I know that if I'm confident and I can stay that way the whole year, then who knows?"

Australia is home to many of the world's top surfers like Mick and Taj, but South American surfers

What's the rope sticking out from Taj Burrows' surfboard? It's a leash that keeps his board from floating away.

hold their own. Victor Ribas was born on November 1, 1971, and learned to surf in the warm waters off his native Brazil. At age 35, Victor is a veteran on the tour and has competed as a pro since 1994. He finished third in the world in 1999 and he was ranked in the Top 20 in 2006. So what is Victor's secret to

Ultimate Surf Spots

Here are five places that are the hottest surf spots in the world for the top pros.

1. Teahupoo, Tahiti (pictured at right): These waves are for experts only. Why? They are the most dangerous in the world. Thick, foamy waves are created when the Pacific Ocean swells up on the coral reefs surrounding the island. "The waves here are the most talked about and the most feared," said Rob Barber, editor of *Carve Surfing* Magazine.

2. North Shore, Oahu, Hawaii: This is the place where surfing was first seen by British explorers in the 1700s. The history, plus the power and size the waves reach here, makes the North Shore a top destination for the pros. "Surfer's reputations are made or lost here," said Barber.

long-term success? He is consistent. Ribas may not be the flashiest or the most daring surfer, but he is in the heart of the competition at almost every event he enters. Victor's consistency year after year is how he has lasted on tour for so many seasons.

▶ 3. Gold Coast, Australia: It is 30 miles of coastline near the city of Brisbane and natives call it "Goldie." Thanks to toasty air and warm water year-round, the Gold Coast is always filled with surfers. Gigantic waves also make it a hot spot.

▶ 4. Jeffrey's Bay, South Africa: J-Bay, located between the cities of Cape Town and Durban, can be super windy, but that makes the surfing more fun. At the section of break called "Supertubes," waves can reach up to 200 yards long!

▶ 5. Maverick's, Half Moon Bay, California: Located between San Francisco and Santa Cruz, waves here can reach 50 feet high. Only the best and bravest of the big-wave riders attempt to tame the Maverick Monsters.

CHAPTER 3

Look for the Girls in the Curl!

THINK SURFING IS ONLY A MALE SPORT? THINK again. Women have been riding the waves alongside the men since the early days in Hawaii. The first surfer in Australia was a woman, Isabel Letham. Isabel rode tandem with Hawaiian legend Duke Kahanamoku when he introduced the sport in her home country in the early 1900s. Today, just like the men, women compete for big cash prizes on the ASP World Tour.

The most successful has been Layne Beachley, who was born on May 24, 1972, in Sydney, Australia, the place she still calls home. Layne grew up surfing, but it wasn't easy being one of a few female surfers surrounded by guys. The male surfers used to try to intimidate her.

Layne Beachley not only has a great name for a surfer, but she has won more world titles than any other woman.

"It was threatening to be a woman who was confident and determined in the water," Layne told *Sports Illustrated* in 2004.

Today, Layne rules the ocean turf. Although her moves aren't as powerful as most men, she is more graceful. Layne appears to dance on top of the water when she catches a wave. Beachley has been on the pro tour since 1997, and won the world championship a women's record six times from 1998 to 2003.

"Self-belief is the secret of success," Layne said. "Set a goal, put your mind to it, and believe it can be done."

Layne's toughest competition in the water comes from Sofia Mulanovich. Sofia was born in Lima, Peru, on June 24, 1983. In 2004, she became the first world champion—male or female—from South America.

"When I was a little kid I used to dream about this," said Mulanovich after her title win. Sofia finished second in 2005, but however she finishes in future events, Sofia will always be proud of her 2004 title, and what it means to be from South America.

"I've done this for my country and for all South Americans," Mulanovich said. "Just to make a change and give them hope."

Keala Kennelly is another woman surfer who is confident enough to go after her dreams. She was born in Kauai, Hawaii, on August 13, 1978. By age five, she was already winning surfing trophies. Keala grew up learning from the best in Kauai—Andy and Bruce Irons.

In 2005, Keala did something that no other woman surfer has done. She was pulled out by a jet-ski into the dangerous reef break off Tahiti. A few moments later, she emerged out of the water **stoked**, safe, and happy.

"Keala, she rules out there," said Bruce Irons after she accomplished her amazing feat. "I don't think any other girl can touch her, she has been the most daring and gung-ho. She really is **radical** out there and no one will get her if [the wave] is over two feet."

Sofia Mulanovich brings a tremendous spirit, along with amazing surfing skills, to her quest for another world title.

CHAPTER 4

Who Are the Next Surf Stars?

TODAY, SURFING IS AS POPULAR AS EVER. AS MUCH as fans would love to have guys like Kelly Slater and Bruce and Andy Irons compete forever, they just won't. So who are the hot young surfers who will be the next Kelly or Bruce or Layne? Here are a couple "grommets" (for more surfing slang, see the box on page 29) to keep an eye on.

John John Florence's name is worth repeating. The 13-year-old was born on October 18, 1992, in Honolulu, Hawaii. When he was six months old, his mom put a life jacket on him and sat him on the nose of a surfboard. He started surfing on his own when he was five years old. In 2005, John John really made news. He became the youngest competitor ever in the world's premier big-wave series, the 2005 Vans

Young John John Florence, 13, is making waves while riding them, amazing older surfers with his skills.

The Comeback Kid

Bethany Hamilton is an up-and-coming surfing star living in Kauai, Hawaii. Born in 1990, by the time she was five, she was already on a board. She was sure she was going to be a pro surfer one day. Then on October 31, 2003, her life changed forever.

Hamilton was in the ocean and lying on her surfboard. She was waiting for the next set of waves to come along. Suddenly, a tiger shark attacked. He bit off her entire left arm just below the shoulder. Although she was bleeding profusely, Bethany paddled to the shore using her right arm. A friend's father rushed her to the hospital, but she still lost 70 percent of her blood that morning.

After such a scary incident, most people would give up surfing forever. Not Bethany. Ten days after

Triple Crown of Surfing in Hawaii.

Only more big things are ahead for this little guy. He says he practices twice a day—before and after school. He already has advice for other young kids who want to start surfing.

"Just practice as much as you can," John John told the *St. Petersburg Times* in 2005. "If you just stick with she lost her arm, Bethany was back out in the water. She taught herself how to paddle and stand up on her board using only one arm.

"When I got up on my first wave, I rode it all the way into the shore, and after that, I just had tears of happiness, I was so stoked to be back," Bethany wrote in her book, *Soul Surfer*.

Today, Bethany is back competing and dreaming of becoming a pro surfer. After surviving a shark attack, becoming a pro should be easy.

"People I don't even know come up to me. I guess they see me as a symbol of courage and inspiration," wrote Bethany.

it and have as much fun as you can, within a few years you'll be super good."

If the talk is about super good surfers, then Carissa Moore is a name that must be mentioned. Carissa, age 14, is the top young female surfer in the world. The young Hawaiian already made history in August of 2006 when she won the 14-and-under

Carissa Moore loves to win, but like a true surfer, she hits the waves because she loves it, not just to win trophies.

boys division on the fifth stop of the 2006 Rip Curl GromSearch. After she blew away the competition, contest director Darren Brilhart said, "This is what it must have been like watching Kelly Slater come up."

Fans and fellow surfers are calling Carissa a future world champ. What does Carissa think?

"I'm just going to hang out and surf and stuff," she says. "Why would I do anything else?"

Surfers would agree with her 100 percent.

Surf Speak

Here are some common surfing terms to help you feel at home in the swell.

Bail   To abandon a board or jump off. A surfer usually bails to avoid a bad crash.

Barrel   A hollow wave that allows the surfer to tuck inside the cylinder

Boost   To get airborne

Carve   A fluid turn while on the board

Chop   Description of a small wave that is created by wind

Face   The front part of the wave

Grommet   A young surfer who is respected, but still needs time to learn

Hang 10   This is when a surfer has all ten toes on the nose of the board

Lineup   The place in the water where surfers wait for the waves.

Ripping   Pulling off an awesome move on a wave

Rip Tide   Ocean flow that has a strong out going current

Shred   Surf very well with lots of back-and-forth movement

Slammed   When a wave knocks a surfer off his board and drills him deep into the water

Snaking   When a surfer catches a wave in front of another surfer who is close to the breaking part of the wave. It is also called cutting off.

Swell   The wavy motion of the open sea

Tow In   Being towed into waves by a boat. The waves are usually too big to surf on any other way.

Zoo   A crowded surfing lineup

GLOSSARY

big air a slang term for a surfing move in which the surfer jumps out of the water on the board before landing back on the wave

Down Under a nickname for Australia

hamstring the tendon that is attached to the large muscle at the back of the upper leg

heirs people who receive something from someone who has died, or, in this case, retired or left a sport

motivation the inspiration a person needs to achieve a goal

qualified in sports, earning a spot on a tour or in a league through other competition

radical surfing slang for "excellent"

stoked very excited and enthused

BOOKS

Luna Bay (series)
By Fran Lantz
New York, Harper Entertainment, various
This fiction series features the adventures of a group of girl surfers.

Soul Surfer
By Bethany Hamilton
New York, MTV Books, 2006
The young girl surfer who lost an arm in a shark attack (see page 26) tells the story of how she overcame the injury and returned to her first love—surfing.

Surfer Girl: A Guide to the Surfing Life
By Sanoe Lake with Steven Jarrett
New York, Little Brown, 2005
Aimed at female surfers, this book covers the history of the sport, equipment you can use, and safety tips.

Surfing
By Tim Rainger
New York, Barron's, 1999
A look at surfing skills, gear, slang, and maneuvers.

WEB SITES

Visit our home page for lots of links about surfing and world surf stars: www.childsworld.com/links

Note to Parents, Teachers, and Librarians: We routinely check our Web links to make sure they're safe, active sites—so encourage your readers to check them out!

INDEX

ABOUT THE AUTHOR

Ellen Labrecque is a former senior editor at *Sports Illustrated for Kids*. She wrote about numerous sports for the magazine and contributed to several *SI Kids* books. She lives in New Jersey with her husband.